BABY BOOK

BABY BOOK

Amy Ching-Yan Lam

Brick Books

Library and Archives Canada Cataloguing in Publication

Title: Baby book / Amy Ching-Yan Lam.
Names: Ching-Yan Lam, Amy, author.
Description: Poems.
Identifiers: Canadiana (print) 20220489459 | Canadiana (ebook)
20220489513 | ISBN 9781771315968 (softcover) | ISBN 9781771315982
(PDF) | ISBN 9781771315975 (EPUB)
Classification: LCC PS8605.H5565 B33 2023 | DDC C811/.6—dc23
2nd edition, October 2023

We gratefully acknowledge the Canada Council for the Arts, the
Government of Canada through the Canada Book Fund, and the Ontario
Arts Council for their support of our publishing program.

Cover image by Tina Guo.
Typeset in Plantin and Times Now.
Design by Victoria Lum.
Author photo by Marvin Luvualu António.
Printed and bound by Coach House Printing.

Brick Books   487 King St. W.
brickbooks.ca   Kingston, ON K7L 2X7

Though much of the work of Brick Books takes place on the ancestral lands
of the Anishinaabeg, Haudenosaunee, Huron-Wendat, and Mississaugas
of the Credit peoples, our editors, authors, and readers from many
backgrounds are situated from coast to coast to coast in Canada on the
traditional and unceded territories of over six hundred nations who have
cared for Turtle Island from time immemorial. While living and working
on these lands, we are committed to hearing and returning the rightful
imaginative space to the poetries, songs, and stories that have been untold,
under-told, wrongly told, and suppressed through colonization.

For my poh-poh,
Yu Kun Ng Tam (1924–2021),
and for my family and friends.

ONE

THE FOUR ONIONS

Four onions express four responses to living.

They're planted in a crinkly pot.

They were cut down to stumps but have now regrown long green blades.

Four floppy hollow shoots.

When the air is hot, blood rushes to the surface of the skin.

When the air is cold, blood rushes into the organs.

This movement can create knowledge.

Changes in temperature can bring about rushes of knowledge.

THE POET LI BAI

In Chinese school I learned a story:

Once there was a very naughty boy. He was lazy and didn't
want to sit around memorizing lessons, so he would skip class
and go to the market instead.

One day, amongst the cabbages and fish heads, he saw an old
woman sitting on an overturned bucket. She was bent over,
slowly grinding a very long and thick iron pole on a stone. Over
and over in circles she kept grinding the pole.

The naughty boy went up to her and said, Hey old woman, what
do you think you're doing?

She said, I need a sewing needle, so I'm making one. It might
take years but I am very determined.

The naughty boy's mouth dropped. This old woman was going
to grind down a six-foot-long pole into a sewing needle.

From that day forward, he never skipped a day of school again.
He became a stellar student and did all of his homework and
memorized all of his lessons.

He went on to become a very successful poet, one of the nation's
most renowned.

From the old lady, he learned the lesson of persistence.

The end.

And the lesson for me?
Like the boy, I didn't want to go to school.
But I also didn't want to become an old woman, doing some
repetitive task.
Why would anyone be impressed by a pole?

We had to recite Li Bai's most famous poem as well.
In the basement classroom we gestured along to the words.

The poet is in his bedroom.

He sees moonlight, like snow, on the floor.

He looks up at the moon.

He looks down and thinks of his home.

Idiotic poem, I thought.
He looks up and then he looks down again?

Still the words echoed all the time in my head.
My head being a parking lot with one car parked in it, and
inside the car, Hello Kitty, Jesus, Qin Shi Huang, and Nelson
Mandela arguing loudly with each other, yelling proverbs and
maxims.

The moon shining brightly on the roof.

Amy! My mom snapped.
She did my Chinese homework while I daydreamed,
writing out the answers for me to copy.
Everything I memorized stayed with me for the quiz day only.

Twenty years later, my mom still has the old Chinese school
notebooks in boxes. A foot massager, a coffee maker, stacked
neatly beside the big Rubbermaids with my old clothing.
She brings out a pair of butter yellow pants that I wore
twenty-one years ago.
She says, Do you want them?
I saved them for you.

The crotch is a bit ripped but the colour is a perfect yellow.
The colour of a disc in the sky.
The colour of a hole where pressure escapes.
I find a needle to mend them.

Then my grandma takes the needle from me.
She shows me a faster stitch.
She shows me a motion that's
not this sequence of events.
Not a fable.
Not a moral.
But a switching
between the inner and outer.

And the old woman in the market talks to herself and to the
lizard under the bucket.
She is describing the movement of the pole.
The dust piling up in spirals.
And the tip, so pointed, it pierces through what's shaping it.

WE PRAY BEFORE DINNER

We pray before dinner.
My grandma starts praying loudly while my uncle is still talking.
She's hungry and she wants to eat.

Dear God, she says, as my uncle is talking about Android phones.
Thank you, God, she says
while he's saying, Samsung camera is—
for the food on the table—
better than iPhone—
and for keeping us all healthy—
and cheaper—
in God's name we pray.
My uncle says, Oops.
My grandma concludes, Amen.
On the television, the Presidential nominee starts saying, You
know, you know the thing—
and then the cuckoo clock goes off.

Koo-koo, koo-koo.
Once my grandma told me, without any warning:
I had twenty brothers and sisters and eighteen of them died.
All dead.
I asked, What! Poh-Poh, how, why?!
She didn't tell me anything else.
She said, I don't know why.
I don't know.
Then she looked at me, her eyes slightly wider, and said,
I know why you're asking me so many questions.
Why?! I said.
She said, Because you want to make a movie of my life!

Oh, I said.

Other facts have been told to me in the same way.

The other day in Chinatown:
A woman with white hair, in soft flowered pants, let out a big
loud sigh.

She leaned herself against a fire hydrant.
She lowered her plastic shopping bags to the ground.
She said, Aiya, so painful!
I went over and asked if she needed help.
She said, No, it's OK, I'd rather walk.
She said, Do you know what the doctor told me?
The doctor said the only option is to chop the leg right off. Yes,
that's what the Western doctor said. And my daughter told me,
If you chop it off I'm not going to push your wheelchair for you.
I said, Oh my god.
She said, I don't want to chop it off! I'd rather walk around in pain.
Your daughter said that?! I asked.
She said, Yes. This is the way human life is.
Then our conversation ended.

At the juice place with yellow walls, the owner talked to me
about Hong Kong.
I had a foamy green juice in my hand.
She said, You're from there? I have an uncle who lives there.
He left Vietnam during the war.
He jumped off the boat as soon as it arrived in the Hong Kong
harbour, he saw cops boarding the boat and he ran away.
He was never registered as a refugee and he never got
documentation.
Now he lives in the city renting a bed somewhere.
You know, one of those cage beds?

I asked, Have you talked to him recently?
She said, No. But I have children and grandchildren and I let
them do whatever they want.
Because otherwise people will kill themselves, she said. Like
one of my nieces.
The girl had to buy a rope.
Can you imagine going out to buy a rope?
Where did she get the rope from?
She said, in conclusion, You can't try to control people, they
will kill themselves.
She said this with certainty.

Back at dinner, the TV continues to play loudly.
After the election coverage, there's a melodrama.

It's about an elderly woman who is dying of cancer.
All of her children died young so she dedicated herself to being
a nanny.
She raised someone else's boy, and she lived very humbly.

The boy is now a wealthy man.
He sits beside her bed.
He regrets not being there for her earlier.
He appeals to God and asks God to save her life.
He cries that there already has been too much suffering.
The old woman looks ahead, his hand in hers.
My sister cries silently.
My mom is crying.
I'm also crying
and my poh-poh looks like she might cry too.

The woman in the movie says,
I don't care about how much suffering there is.
I know how I learned this attitude
and I don't care if it's good or bad.

Steam rises from the food on the table.

There's a platter of choy sum with garlic.
There's a bowl of lotus root soup.
My uncle explains the causes of populism.
A car beep-boops outside.
Then, weeeeeeeeeeeeeeeeeee-oooooooooooooooooo—
splitting loud weeeeeeeeeeeeeeeeeee-oooooooooooooooooo

NATURAL FACT

Taste and smell are the only senses that trigger memory.

So I eat to try to remember my life as a baby.

If I eat what I ate when I was one year old:

- Carrot soup
   - White rice
      - Oatmeal

Then maybe I can remember my memories.

What I wanna know is: what does it feel like to be a baby in the world's most expensive city?

And what does it feel like to be parents raising a baby in the world's most expensive city?

So I eat oatmeal all the time now, but I still kind of hate it.

I remember that, as a teen, I used to argue with my parents every time I had to eat it.

Every morning I would fight with my parents while the oatmeal grew cold on the table.

I would only eat it after it had congealed, while complaining about how it had congealed.

Then when the oatmeal was finally finished, Mom and Dad would go to the restaurant and make meat sauce rotini.

The distinction of "world's most expensive city" can seem like a
natural fact.

"It's so expensive here," said like a fact of nature, like saying,
"It's an island."

Like on the TV show *The Crown*, the characters say,
"Everybody has to make sacrifices"
as if sacrifices are natural facts.

They are deeply unhappy because they have to keep procreating
in a predetermined way.

I'm scared of this idea of sacrifice and what it does in families.

The other day I read a children's book titled *Franklin in the Dark*.

I wonder if my mom ever read it to me.

Franklin the turtle is scared of small, dark places.
He's afraid of the dark inside his own shell.
He's so scared he ties a rope around his shell and drags it
around behind him.
He doesn't like to go in it.

He drags what he's scared of behind him.

Anyway, Franklin goes for a walk. He meets other animals and
asks for help. Unfortunately, they can only offer him things
that are helpful for themselves. A polar bear who is afraid of the
cold offers a snowsuit. A duck who is afraid of deep water offers
water wings. A lion who is afraid of loud noises offers earmuffs.

Franklin wanders home all tired. His mother, scared that he was
lost, gives him a big hug.

He's so sleepy he can't help but crawl into his shell.
He turns a nightlight on, and then he falls asleep inside the shell
with the light on.

The story is amazing because it's about
a fear of your own essence,
or something that defines you.

And in the end, the fear is still there, the turtle doesn't get rid of it.

The fact is that the city became so expensive when a British colonial government laid claim to all of the land, parcelled it out in limited contracts to the highest bidders, and everybody was forced to rent from them.

The fact is that the parents with the baby had to live separately from her so that they could work.
The parents had to sacrifice their time with the baby, in order to raise the baby.

I think I have a memory of the royal family giving up all of their jewels.

A bit of smoke, poof, gone.

The sacrifice and devotion of offering food to the no-longer-living.

A pile of oranges that are eaten from the inside out.

Five beautiful books on a shelf that remain closed.

Each is for a different period of life.

One has bright blue inflatable pages that can float in water.

The second comes with a lock and key.

The third has long horizontal pages that take two people to flip.

The fourth is bound in tinfoil, cardboard, and tape.

The fifth has a cover of mirror-finish gemstone green.

SUNFLOWER SEED

The therapist hit play on the Theta Waves Binaural Beats
YouTube video after I told her, Heh, I dunno, I'm fearful.
She said, Amy, we don't know, and it doesn't matter
where the fear comes from.

All of a sudden, I remembered the photo.
Out of the soup, I saw the photo.

It's a photo of a man standing with his hands behind his back.
My mom told me about it while watching TV.

She said, Do you know how Mah-Mah and Yeh-Yeh got
married? That Mah-Mah never even met him, she was just
given a photo? The photo was of Yeh-Yeh standing with his
hands clasped behind his back and Mah-Mah cried out, *I have
to marry this man with no hands?* She was only sixteen.

The actors on TV were crying around a hospital bed—
I said, frowning, Oh my god, she must have been so scared, she
had to marry a man she didn't know?
My mom said, No, she was just making fun of him!

A character woke up from a coma—
My mom laughed and continued watching the TV show.

She forgot about the photo.
I promptly forgot as well.

This morning I woke up from a dream still stuck in the dream.

I was in a fancy restaurant with a curved wooden bar, sitting
with someone I'm jealous of.
She ate a giant crab that had a head within a head while
I watched.
The crab had a mouth filled with teeth and behind the teeth,
another, smaller head with a mouth filled with more teeth.
It was cooked in a cream sauce with pasta.
She kept saying, Yum, so delicious, do you want to try a bite?
without stopping chewing.

Apparently there is an evolutionary tendency towards crabs, and
several crustaceans have, independently of each other, become
crabs.

I felt very uncomfortable in the dream because I had a new
piercing of a steak knife hanging from my throat.
Then all day I've had the feeling of a hole in my throat.

There is a path from perception to testimony, or from
experience to story.
The path is loopy and has many holes, but also has parts that
are the opposite of holes.

For example, there was an experiment with people whose visual
cortexes are damaged but not their eyes.
Their eyes perceive visual information but it can't be processed.

In this experiment, the subjects sat in front of a painting of a
sunflower.

When asked, Is there a painting here?
The subjects said, I don't know.
But when asked, If there *were* a painting, what would it be of?
Some of them said, Oh, a sunflower.

Somehow it's still known, or not-not known.

The opposite of a hole being a fountain or a spring.
The opposite of a path being an enormous, sensitive field.

When I trip, or drop something, I'm usually worrying
about it as I do it.
I don't want to drop this
and then I drop it.

Like when S. lost her metro pass in London, England.
One morning she said, I definitely can't lose this, it's so
expensive!
Then later that day she lost it.

That evening, she said, It's a lesson about what you tell yourself
can or cannot happen to you.
What you can or cannot take.

I think this means, like, don't be scared of accidents.
Or try not to be scared of accidents.
Or try not to be scared of the lack of choice.

There is a half-second delay between perception and consciousness.

A study says that, despite the lag,
We do not feel like we are only watching the movies of our lives.
Or the movies of our parents' or grandparents' lives.

Our brains construct a new timeline of experience for us.

A string of quick looks at the source, or a surfing of the spiral.

The conversion of a series of epiphanies into a series of catastrophes, or the switching of genres from tragedy to comedy.

A glass jar implodes in mid-air, inspiring a waterfall of lentils.

PERSON WATERING FLOWERS

Sunlight cracks heads.

Water arcs from a hose onto flowers.

A man gazes at his yellow chrysanthemums.
He stands completely still while water arcs from the hose.
Each yellow flower is huge compared to its stem.
The fact that they are upright rests
against the fact that the water falls down.

The man stands perfectly still.
He stares at his flowers.

The fact of uprightness comes from sweetness.
I learned this in First Aid.

Taste it and see if it's sweet, he says.
The way you can tell if the fluid around the brain is leaking out
is if you taste it, and it's sweet, the First Aid instructor says.

Because the brain swims in a sticky sugar syrup.
This syrup helps take some of the weight off the neck.

Otherwise our brains would be too heavy, he demonstrates,
bringing his chin down to his chest.
Touch the fluid between your forefinger and thumb to see if it's
sticky and then taste it, he says.
He walks around the classroom with his chin on his chest.

In my apartment there's a mouse who eats only ashes.
And only special ashes: only the ashes of sandalwood incense.

I put poison out because I want it to stop eating my ashes.
I read the label carefully, looking for the promise that the mouse
will not die indoors.
I find the promise I'm looking for:
THE MOUSE WILL ONLY DIE OUTDOORS.

In the basement classroom there's been a mass casualty incident. All eight of us students have been stabbed by ballpoint pens, all in the same place on our legs.
We tie tourniquets around our legs.
The instructor says, NEVER take the tourniquet off, EVER!

Because enzymes from rotting flesh will travel to other parts of the body, rotting the living parts as well. There is no pain in the rotting, only in the living.

Bonk, bonk bonk.

The sun bangs against cars, asphalt, lampposts.

The types of pain I am most familiar with are:
- sharp, nauseating
or
- tender, kneading

Air bounces off my head.

It was the best thing I ever did, he says.
The First Aid instructor tells us the story of the best thing he ever did.

He worked as a family doctor in Iran before moving to Canada. His practice was in a small town and once he sewed four toes back onto a foot by himself, without the proper equipment, at two in the morning.
The toes came in a bucket filled with ice and he had to figure out which one went where. He was scared, he didn't know if it would work.

You actually need a plastic surgery microscope for the veins, he says.

But it worked.
One day the person showed up unannounced with a friend and
pastries and a bouquet and thanked him.

...Two-thousand-year-old fragment of a sculpture of
a fist holding a flower...

Thank you to sweetness tied up.
Thank you to sweetness smashed and tied up.
Thank you to sweetness smashed into dust.

TWO

LAND MADE OF FOOD

In the beginning, the ground was the milk of beans,
until it was boiled and squeezed into tofu.

Then hot sauce shot up from below and filled up the seas.

Rocks appeared—peanuts.

Then trees
with leaves of roasted nori
and trunks of nougat.

When it rains, it rains perogies.

THE PEOPLE'S DREAM

The artist residency in "New England" sent an email with the
subject line:
WE ARE REMOVING "COLONY" FROM OUR NAME.
Now it will be named after its founder only, no colony.

One time at dinner there I told my story of going on a $99
week-long bus tour in Sichuan, China.
I went with my family, we thought it was a good deal.

My dad was the first to vomit.
He waved off my advice about drinking more water. I felt very
upset with him, like I blamed him for getting sick.
Before long everyone on the tour bus had food poisoning.
The tour guide kept smiling at the front of the bus, ignoring the
sounds of retching.

We were brought to a tea museum.
We watched a presentation about local tea and then were
quickly ushered from the small display area into a giant gift
shop. We were left in the shop for several hours, or until enough
sales were made.

Then we were brought back on the buses.
The buses drove for exactly 1.5 minutes to the other side of the
parking lot. We were at the silk museum.
Again we were led into the gift shop. Again we were left there
for hours, until a salesperson cried, and the retired man from
California from Hong Kong, green in the face, gave in and
bought a silk comforter for $400 USD.

Then we were driven to another restaurant that looked exactly
like the restaurant we ate at the previous night, and the night
before. Same menu items and tablecloths and chair coverings
but different buildings, different locations, different people.
No person who was not North American Chinese ever eating at
any of these restaurants, no smaller group than two busloads of
people at a time ever entering these restaurants.

The man from California vomited on the doorstep.
Following the lead of our smiling tour guide, the rest of us
stepped over the vomit puddle to go into the restaurant.
Many plates of food were brought to the tables even though no
one was hungry.

Afterwards we got back on the buses.
And this repeated every day for the rest of the week.

Halfway through the trip I saw a statue, newly erected, of
"Han and Tibetan Friendship." I then realized we were
participating in a colonial government project, in Tibetan and
Qiang territory.

I tell this story and everybody at dinner at the fancy place in
America is laughing, loud laughter all around the table.

One man says you should write about it for *Harper's*.
At the table there are a few people who have actually written for
Harper's and they agree. It's a great story.
I feel embarrassed and focus on my lamb chop,
pan-seared, with rosemary.
I feel embarrassed for telling a story they enjoy so much.
I should have complicated it with references to American or
Canadian projects.
The American, the Canadian, the Chinese Dreams.

I should have included that our smiling tour guide survived the
Sichuan earthquake of 2008, which happened while she was
working on a bus.

But it's time for dessert.
Vanilla strawberry shortcake on a crisp white platter is delivered
by a high school student.
Beside it, a mound of whipped cream in a bowl.
The folds of cream gently absorbing light.

The night is rich, soft.
I walk back to my little cottage studio in the woods.

The sky, the buildings, they all have the perfect texture.
Everything is absorbent.

In order to fall asleep.

In order to fall asleep it helps to imagine myself as someone
else, someone with an entirely different set of issues, a set that is
knowable, contained, enumerated on a list.

When I was eleven, in order to fall asleep, I would imagine
myself as a thirteen-year-old White boy. He was the main
character in a book called *Hatchet* that I got from the library.

His small plane crashes and he's left alone in the
"Canadian" wilderness.
He has to learn how to survive by himself.
The only tool he has is a hatchet.
He eats berries and turtle eggs and makes fish traps out of sticks
and grass.
Nature around him is scary but he overcomes it.

I would sleep in his cave carved by water out of rock,
surrounded by little piles of dried berries, fish, eggs.

I would count each pile before sleep.
I would list each precious item.
Then I would fall asleep and dream his dreams.

A country-blue house in a cul-de-sac at 3:00 a.m.

The highway loops around it.

There are gases that are scented to not be odourless.

There are gases that are odourless.

In order to fall asleep I am someone putting together a
Christmas tree.
A fake one from a crumpled cardboard box.
Each branch is made of twisted grey metal and plasticky
fabric needles.
The trunk is painted not brown but green, to be more hidden.
It's hollow with little pockets, where the metal branches
are inserted.
The interior metal tip of each branch is daubed with paint to
label where it goes in the trunk.
Yellow means bottom of the tree (the biggest), red is middle of
the tree (smaller), blue is the top (smallest).

And the very top branch, the one that sticks straight up, that the
star or angel sits on, does it have a paint daub, or is it obvious?

It's obvious.

It's loose, not yet put in place, starless, angel-less. Lying loose on the dusty rose carpet.

When completed, in the dream, the tree is turned upside down and ignited.

DRAWING OF THE RAIN

I drew the rain as little grey lines.

It rained all day and night and everything was grey.
Water fell through the sky continuously.
Its motion made everything seem especially still.

My drawing looks like a square with lines on top of it.
It doesn't look continuous.
I wonder if the rain will escape from the drawing.

I say this because apparently the devil can escape from
a painting.
Someone painted a mural for a church and they had to paint the
devil three times.
The first two times it disappeared from the painting
overnight...
Somehow the background remained uninterrupted.
The third and final time, the painter painted it
chained by the neck.
Then the devil stayed.

I don't know how to tie up the rain.

I think that when the devil escaped
and the background filled itself in
the painter should have honoured
and preserved the background.

ENGLISH ACCENT

On Remembrance Day, our teacher organized a letter-writing
contest.
A World War II veteran came to our class and talked
to us. He was an old White man in an army uniform with a
maroon beret.
We sat on the floor with our legs crossed.
He told us of men clambering through ditches with mud-filled
boots, separated from their families,
suffering for freedom.
Afterwards we were told to write a letter to him, to thank him
for his service, and for talking to us.

I wrote a few paragraphs by hand on lined paper. I tried to make
the sentences worthy of such an important topic, to convey its
tragedy, evoke its ideals, conclude on hope, and so on.

About a week later, it was announced that I had won
the contest.
The veteran wrote me back, thanking me for my letter,
for listening.
I filled with shame.
I had only written the words because they sounded good.
I didn't really care about the veteran or the war.
I just knew that World War II was a big deal
and I knew how to be eloquent in English about it.

After winning the writing award I tell my mom about it on the
way to swimming class.
She says, Good job Amy.
During the class, we fetch bricks from the bottom of the pool.
The bricks are rough and heavy. I struggle on the way up,
kicking against the water, arms sinking with the brick, trying
not to drop it.

My mom picks us up after the lesson.
She drives my sister and me everywhere.
We sit with wet hair and frost on the car windows.
Drive for thirty minutes to piano lessons where we perform
Bach sonatas. Then drive for another forty-five minutes to
drama class where we recite Shakespeare monologues. *Is this a
dagger...?*
And then drive for another seventy minutes to the concert hall
for competition.

We perform the classics of romance and revenge.
We march out from the wings to applause.
The judges award us with medals: gold, silver, bronze.

To become a master of English literature, you have to learn this medieval English story about a guy selling forgiveness.

The pardoner wears a little hat on his head and he has a box full of bones.
He says they're the bones of saints, and if you give him $100 you can buy one, dip it in the well, and be forgiven by God.

The bones are just pig bones he got from the butcher shop.
But he is a convincing storyteller, and he talks persuasively about correct behaviour.
His speech is mellifluous, honeyed, stirring.
If the listener is smart enough they won't be taken in by him.
But even if the listener is a sucker, a pig-bone buyer, salvation still reaches them.

The English church says salvation cannot be impeded by the people it passes through. Not by a colonizer, not by a liar.

This week I am learning about the truth of expression.

My teacher says that if you smile, even when you are feeling sad,
you can still receive some of the benefits of being happy.
Even if you are simply smiling while sad.
He says that shame is similarly a physiological reaction.
It exists in your body and you can get rid of it with a physical
action.

You imagine someone passing a hot potato straight from a pot
of boiling water to you, burning your hand.
Your palm is facing up, the potato is placed in it, and then you
flip your hand so it falls out.

We do this together in a circle with a selenite lamp
in the middle.
I stare into the selenite lamp and drop the hot potato.
The potato falls to the floor with a thunk.
The teacher says, It's proof that your actions can help you
change your feelings.

Last night I read a novel by a well-liked White American author, lauded as his best yet.
The novel is based on his personal experiences.
There's a section about a family story.
The protagonist's grandfather was an American diplomat in Taiwan, after World War II, and his father went to a fancy International school there, with other diplomats' sons.
One day, they goaded a classmate into shooting and killing all of the cows in a local farmer's field.

Upon finding his cows dead in the field, the farmer went to the school.

He started yelling in the lobby.

He demanded an explanation.

He wanted an apology.

He refused to leave.

The story ends with the father saying, *I don't remember what happened beyond the fact that the kids made fun of the farmer in mock-Chinese...*

And the farmer was dragged away by the police.

Decades of no apologies or fake ones.

Decades of art about war.

Art that is fluent, rhetorically successful.

A beautifully carved wooden box.

That which blocks the truth is physical.

It's a hot, stuck feeling in the body.

It's a heavy heat. It's a heavy box.

The physical remains physical.

The physical can be moved.

The physical can be destroyed.

When destroyed, it doesn't disappear.

But it can be moved.

THREE

ROOM WITH NO DOOR

Someone has an opinion about what other people deserve.

They keep this opinion on the floor.

It is made of polished brass, rectangular, about a metre long.

On the other side of the room, there is a pole mounted horizontally near the ceiling.

Balanced along the length of the pole are this person's needs and wants.

They are spheres made of cast iron.

On the right side of the pole are the needs, and on the left side are the wants.

OUR HOUSE

In the house where I grew up, all the blinds were always drawn.

I go back to open them.

I'm twelve years old, wishing for a new brand-name sweater.

On the weekend my parents make my wish come true.

I look at my new DKNY turtleneck sweater in my room.
I lay it out carefully on the carpet.
The price tag has many clearance stickers and says WINNERS.
It says that forty dollars was saved off the original price.
I feel protected by the savings, the sweaters, the carpet. It's
snowing outside.
We can see outside now.

My dad, forty-two years old, smiles as he passes by, seeing me
looking at my present.
I run downstairs with my new sweater.

My sister is in the kitchen.
She's nine but she works for the bank.
She has to connect over VPN to work from home.
She works fourteen hours a day, peering into her laptop, typing
furiously and sighing. She's very good at her job.

My sister says, I'm going to buy Mom and Dad a house to
retire in.
Then she tells me the amount that's needed.
It's an impossible sum of money.
She says, I'm going to do it.

I clutch my sweater and squeeze tight my eyes, trying to figure
out what stocks to buy or what numbers to pick for the lottery.

Then my sister tells me two stories.

The first is about her co-worker S.

Her co-worker S. had never invited any of them over
before, even though they had been to all of the other co-
workers' homes. Then, after many years, she did. Upon
arriving at the house, she immediately ushered them
downstairs into the basement. They caught only a glimpse
of the upstairs area, which was all bare two-by-fours, torn-
up tiles, half-scraped baseboards. The basement was more
finished, but not entirely. It turned out that they had been
living exclusively in the basement since they had bought
the house five years ago. They had picked the house on the
premise that her husband was going to renovate it, but he
insisted on doing everything himself, refusing any help,
and suffered, getting nothing done. It was like she was
tired of hiding it, my sister says, and we were all silent in
the car home.

The second is about our Auntie E.

Auntie E. would take us out shopping when we went back to Hong Kong as kids. She was always the coolest aunt, the most free, she was rumoured to have a White boyfriend, she spoke English the best. If we needed to use the toilet while we were out, she would take us to the lobby of a fancy hotel and have us walk in like we were guests. She never married and the last time I saw her, she was wearing purple head-to-toe. Now, my sister says, she used up all of her savings, she has no more money, she's almost seventy, she can't afford her apartment, she has to move out soon, and in a city like Hong Kong. The other aunts are trying to help but she doesn't answer her phone and she says different things to different people when she does. My sister says, No one knows what the actual situation is, or how to help her.

Still clutching my sweater, I take these stories from my sister.
I don't want her to hold them anymore.

A giant puppy guards our house, running around the yard.

I guess I can feed the stories to the puppy.

I wave them at him and he comes, leaping through a window
and crashing through the glass to slide across the floor.

He swallows the stories in one gulp.

Then he pins my head with one paw and my sister's with the
other. He tickles us until we give up, or until he's tired and
doesn't want to play anymore.

PROTECTION

The opportunity to have ANY DESIRE MADE REAL was
given to a person.

The astrologer told this story on his podcast.

The lucky person asked to experience the vastness of God.
Their wish was granted, but the experience of vastness was
hellish and terrifying.
They begged to be released.
Finally, to their relief, God re-appeared, in the form of
a baby with both its big toes in its mouth.

God is personal, the astrologer said.
Terrifying and also personal, like a baby.

Then at dinner Emerson talked about his neighbours who
caught a mouse.
They found it so cute, they didn't want to kill it or exile it, so
they put it in a gerbil cage, fed it treats, and named it "Friday."
But then they had to move to another country.
They couldn't take the mouse with them, so they tried to give it
to the Humane Society. The Humane Society said,
We don't take mice.
So then they tried to set the mouse free, but by that time it
didn't want to leave the cage, it didn't want to go.

At night in bed I thought, Oh God, please help me.

Please protect me and my family.

Protect us from the hellishness of society.

Imagining a tent made of yellow light, sheltering me and my family.

Then I liked a Pornhub account with videos of fucking a "crystal" pussy.

A dick fucks an ice cube that's soft and wet and room temperature.

You can see the dick through the transparent walls, from the side, which is different than the usual view.

For sure I'm made horny by fear and by dreaming.
Every time I wake up from a dream I'm horny.
Especially if it's a scary dream.

I read that dreams are used to cement memories.
This is part of the path from perception to testimony, or from
experience to story.

Dreams associate sensorial details or cues with memories.
*The more bizarre, dramatic, and absurd the cue, the more resilient is
the memory with which the cue has been associated.*

(There's the implicit assumption that the dream is more absurd
or unbelievable than the history.)

Last night the dream was of visiting a professor's nice house, so nice that even the air had a nice texture, a special "textured air." But upon going to the bathroom I discovered a back room where people were kept in fish tanks like those at the grocery store. The tanks were filled with ice.

Both my mom and sister got splashed in the face by fish in tanks at the grocery store the other week.
And there are prisons.

It's personal.

It's personified.

It's a person
walking down the street
wearing a grey T-shirt that says

LIFE NOT WORTH LIVING

The person doesn't even know where they got the T-shirt from.
Maybe it was free.

The terror of the world personified.
The person casually walking.

Casual like the categories:
1) What to protect
2) What does not need protection, and can be expended or
discarded

These categories can justify holding what you love very, very
close.

At the park, extra horny, we saw a sculpture of a polar bear made of white, plastic garbage.

It was standing on an iceberg made of blue plastic garbage.

The sign said, *THE ICE IS MELTING — REDUCE, REUSE, RECYCLE, REFUSE.*

They added the fourth, new *R*.

A kid walking by said, exasperated, Ya, of course I've already seen that bear, like a million times!

The kid understands that his interests have been pitted against the bear's.

A child vs. the bear.

A baby vs. everyone else.

The bear vs. the family.

The family vs. all else.

Then down the path, a special cow with a wet nose.
We stood close to the fence and murmured to it,
You're so nice, what a nice cow.
It had floppy red fur covering its eyes and its knees.

It's innocent.
The innocent cow.
The big, innocent cow.
The innocence is so big, it can't be believed.

PINK OUTFIT

There's a landlord in France who always wears pink, to calm
people down.

He specializes in buying buildings that are being squatted: he
tells the previous owners that their buildings are not worth the
hassle, better to have the money, etc., and then he gets rid of the
squatters.

The colour of his shirt and pants is directed at the frustrated
owners as he offers a sum that's much less than what they want,
and at the angry squatters as he harasses them in their homes.
It's also directed at himself, in the mirror.

The colour has been proven to be calming as measured through
physiological changes.

Blood rushing, or sweating.
Throat and gut twisting.
Ass clenching.

The last time I was lied to (that I know of):
A smiling managerial person in a conflict-resolution meeting
said, I'm sorry, some things were just out of our control.
We want to move forward.

If you chew a bunch of pink Pepto-Bismol chewable tablets,
they will turn your tongue grey-black.

The official name for this temporary condition is "black hairy
tongue."

Truth can't be measured through physiological changes.
Lie detectors don't detect lies, but fear.
Lie detectors aren't reliable because a person can be fearless
when lying.

A monochrome outfit says seeker, certified, protected.

At the gym the monks all had maroon sneakers.

The sneakers were the exact same shade as their robes.

Before lunch I bought some muted dark green sweatpants.
As a kid I was told, Looking at green is good for the eyes, look
out into the distance at the trees, it's good for your eyesight.

The colour can change your eyes.

The last time I lied was in saying I felt better than I did.
It kind of worked.

The scary part is that it kind of works.

Like a system that straddles something closed
to suck all the air out of it and replace it with new air.

The system kind of works.

In other recent news, they've announced a new instrument:
It measures the fuckable,
or fuckability.
It's very sensitive.
The scale starts at "Desirable" and goes all the way to
"Indestructible."

LIFE'S NOT FAIR

Is something that people I know and love believe.

During dinner, a news show from Hong Kong plays.

On the table is fried rice noodle with beef.

The TV news host is "investigating" people panhandling on the streets.

The camera zooms in on the dishes the panhandlers use to collect money.

The host asks, Why are all the dishes covered with plastic bags? What is the meaning of the plastic bag? Is the plastic bag the sign of a system of organization, gang membership?

The host finds a woman who has been panhandling in two different locations on two different days. She jabs the microphone in the woman's face.
Why did you say this yesterday?
And why do you say this today?
There are inconsistencies in your story.

The show accuses the people of pretending to panhandle: They don't need the money.

These people are hazards to pedestrians, the host says. They take up areas of the sidewalk and people have to walk around them.

The host concludes the segment behind a desk that is a rounded, reflective plastic shape, on top of a platform of a similar shape, in front of a wall of more rounded shapes of varying heights and depths.

69

The story she's just told is a variation of "God Pretends to Be a Beggar."

It expresses that suffering is not only extremely virtuous, but that its consequences are not truly experienced.

It perpetuates the image of God as poor, and the poor as liars.

Then, on another TV channel, Canadian, the archbishop says that they haven't completed the accounting of their wrongs.
They don't have the time and resources right now.
They're hoping to do it.
He speaks from a modest-looking office.

All of this happens while the noodles cool on the table.

The action of believing is related to the action of eating and the action of fucking.

These actions require using the whole body.

These actions require the entire body.

The universe is not made by God, but God is made by the universe.

In the sixteenth century, a person was executed for spreading this idea. He said that:

> *In the beginning, there was chaos, which was like a big sea of milk.*
>
> *It churned and churned, until it became cheese.*
>
> *Then, in the cheese, worms appeared, which were the angels.*
>
> *And among these angels was God.*

The man also said that the rich exploited the poor. He himself was poor.

He was persecuted over decades, undergoing multiple trials and sentences.

He couldn't let go of the story about the worms.
He kept telling it to people, even after years of punishment, even as he promised not to.
So he was killed.

The bishops laughed at him, incredulous.

Now everybody laughs at the book titled:

MASTURBATE YOUR WAY TO MILLIONS

It's ranked #29,332 in Self-Help Books.

It can't be that easy.
If only it were that easy!

You can't masturbate your way to wealth, and the universe isn't made of cheese.

Except if you can, and
if it is.

Cuz the church has profited from everyone masturbating.

One time I masturbated stiffly in the chapel on a pew.
That session was worth $2.
All the other ones $1.

I'm expecting my money back.

I'm also owed for all the years I stopped praying.

Everybody is owed for all their unsaid prayers.

Thousands of angels on their bellies, moaning.

POPULAR SONG

There's a hit song about my mother's former part-time job at a country club.

It's called "Fuck the Summer Club."

The three verses detail what I find unacceptable about the context.

The first verse is about the club's $50,000 joining fee.

The chorus sounds like a Christmas carol.

This is a song known and sung by everyone!

It drifts through the streets, out of car windows, alongside the exhaust.

DOOR

Ron lived without a front door on his apartment for over a month (as an artwork).

He took it off its hinges.

People stole from him, but not "that" much, he said, or not as much as you would think.

FOUR

AUTOICON

Some trees are pruned until they look like lumpy forks.
This method is called pollarding.
Their branches are cut year after year to stay at the same height,
becoming thick and stocky, unmoved by wind.

I walked past a series of pollarded trees on my way to the
library. A cold breeze blew, the trees remained still.

The talk at the library was about a project called *AUTOICON*
by the artist Donald Rodney.
It is a representation of himself as an interactive
computer program.
An attempt to make an immortal version of himself
and a proposition about what an artist supposedly is.
Or what a person supposedly is.

Donald Rodney never got to see the project completed.
He died from a chronic illness at the age of thirty-six in 1998.
He had been working on the idea with his friends.
After his death, his friends made it for him.

I interacted with *AUTOICON* on a laptop at the library.
It loaded slowly from the disk.
I typed Hello
and *AUTOICON* responded with a small, fuzzy
black and white image of a strangely angled street.

It felt special to be in the presence of someone living on after
death, fuzzy and slow.

At University College London there is a skeleton in an outfit
that sits in a glass box.

It is the autoicon of Jeremy Bentham, a patron of the university,
and inventor of a type of prison and the word "autoicon."
Donald Rodney studied art there and had to walk by it often.

Jeremy Bentham's skeleton is dressed in his clothes, padded
with hay, sitting on a chair, posed as if "in thought."
Whoever stuffed it didn't put enough hay in the pants, and the
hands, represented by a pair of stiff leather gloves, are way too big.
It's topped with a wax head with shiny eyes wearing a hat.
I imagine Donald looking at it and laughing.

Jeremy Bentham's autoicon was originally intended to have
his actual mummified head, but it was too off-putting, so they
made the wax head instead.

Jeremy Bentham thought his autoicon to be an improved version
of a statue.

A few of Donald Rodney's friends were at the library that
breezy day.
They had helped make his *AUTOICON*.
We were crammed in a small room around a very big table.
They said that some of the frustrating, or opaque, or tricky,
qualities of *AUTOICON* come from it being a piece of software
from the 90s, but others came from Donald.
They said that the process of making it was not easy, that there
were disagreements.

I found this to be beautiful, that these friends mourned and
made Donald's idea together.
That they argued while making it.
That the mourning contained disagreement.
The difficulty or complexity reflected in their friendship.

Months later I'm at my desk with a bowl of cold pasta. The outside air is the same temperature as the water from the tap.

I read about Donald Rodney's last exhibition, *Nine Night in Eldorado*, which he made after the death of his father.
I read that "Nine Night" refers to a period of mourning in the Caribbean. I read that Eldorado refers to a mythical land of plenty (England).

I look at a photo of a work in the show.
It's an empty wheelchair, a maroon leather seat with wires and sensors on the metal frame.
The sensors are programmed so that the wheelchair can navigate by itself around people, walls, furniture, etc.
The wheelchair could go to gallery openings when Donald was unable to attend, when he was sick, or unwilling, or for other private reasons.

His absence made visible
or his absence made non-negotiable.
His absence made autonomous.

The title of the autonomous wheelchair is *Psalms*.

I google "most famous psalm" to try to remember the one
I know.
The first result is the one I recognize from church as a teenager.

> *You prepare a table before me in the presence of my enemies.*
> *You anoint my head with oil; my cup overflows.*
> *Surely goodness and love will follow me all the days of my life.*

The words remind me of the soup made from leftover iceberg
lettuce served at Bible camp and the hot boys playing acoustic
guitars around a fire.
I sing them very seriously, holding a Styrofoam cup of watery
broth and shivering.

I still feel moved by this singing to the spirit.

This singing together while feeling alone.

At the first funeral I ever went to there were people being
very loud.
It was a great-uncle's funeral, the entrance lined with large
arrangements of big blooming flowers, rows of portraits of him
on stands, surrounded by more flowers.

There were mourners I did not recognize, in white, with burlap
sashes and white hats.
They were crying very loudly, right in the middle of everyone.

I was confused by the white outfits and by the crying.
The wails were so loud it seemed staged.
The wailing so loud it seemed insincere.
I thought they must have been paid, professional mourners.

I felt so embarrassed, to watch the crying, to be paid to cry,
an embarrassing tradition, tacky. *Lo tow*, the Cantonese word
for tacky, vulgar, gaudy, ugly, gross.

But I was wrong!
My mom says that there were no professional mourners there,
that the people in the outfits were close family members.

My sister says, Haha Amy! That was real sadness!
They weren't paid!

Oops, I confused it with what I thought Chinese people do.

And now that I think about it:
Even if they were paid.

Their performance of wailing allowed others to join in, to be
less visible, less burdened, more free.

Alone in a physical place:

The wind blows through leaves and I wonder, what is wind, and why is it so amazing.

Hello world
and
Hello spirit

Sometimes people allow spirit to flow through them.

Many red, crumpled faces shaking out of sync.

FIVE

FORCE

A growing pepper faces the sky.

A drooping flower pushes against the earth.

IRON POLE

A person nearing what other people said was the end of her life
had an idea.

Or she experienced an idea:
it came to her fully formed.

She pulled two chairs and a long, hollow pole out of her
overstuffed closet and took them down to the road that ran
through the town.
She set up the two chairs in the middle of the road.
She sat down on one of them.
She held onto one end of the pole.
The other end rested on the other chair.

She put her mouth on the end of the pole in her hand
and exhaled forcefully into it.
The pole glowed baby blue.

Eventually a car drove up, honking.

She said, Nope, you cannot pass.

In order to pass, she had a specific set of instructions (which
can't be disclosed).

The car kept honking.
She repeated herself until the car turned around,
the driver cursing.

She said, That's what it is.
It's non-negotiable.
It came to me like this and I received it as it is.

DEMANDS

"Peacefully" or "peaceful" are words used to praise people as they make demands.

Everywhere people make demands in public.

Peaceful like calm, harmonious, bloodless.

Level, quiet, equable.

Tranquil, composed, mellow.

This allows the demands to be smooth, undisturbed, neutral.

Everywhere demands are described as if they're words in stone tablets.

Carved, heavy, fixed.

The people have spoken.

In this way the demands are removed from their sources.

When, actually, the people are speaking.

People are arguing, people are suffering, people are arguing over suffering.

People are desiring, people are sharing their desires, people are getting explicit about their desires.

People are getting really explicit.

At the end of a documentary about the painter Bhupen Khakhar, there's a shot of him lying on his bed,
looking at an open window with a curtain.

He describes how he would paint this room he's in, how he would capture the movement of the curtain by the wind.

Bhupen says,

> We forget our duty towards ourselves. What we should do in life and in art is do exactly what one likes. The difficulty may be to find out what one likes.

And, also,
the difficulty may be to find the people you like and what they like.
Like, EXACTLY what they like.

In another use of peacefully:

The curtain and the wind move peacefully.

They refuse to be stilled.

I learned recently that the early colonial British courts in Hong Kong had difficulty with the concept of perjury for Chinese people.

The British did not believe that Chinese people could commit to telling the truth, even with a special Chinese oath, performed without a Bible.

The British did not believe that the Chinese could conceive of an afterlife, and so concluded that they could not take any binding oaths.

This meant that Chinese people could not commit perjury, because they were incapable of understanding the true consequences of lying under oath.

Therefore they could not be punished for lying, nor could they be trusted to tell the truth about anything that happened.

Some of the first letters I wrote were apologies. They were demanded by my dad as punishment.

The first was to the teacher for being late.
The second was to my dad, for taking five dollars from his wallet.

I wrote them in pencil on lined paper, in English, and folded them up.

My dad read them and said, OK.

Recently, I learned of a very important letter he had to write to the British government in Hong Kong, near the end of its rule, to ensure our survival.

I learned about it decades after it happened.

The elected official invited my friends and I to a meeting after we sent a letter with demands.

I was worried about forgetting my facts and numbers on racism and "unaffordability."
The meeting was on Halloween.
I found myself telling him a joke.
I said cheerily, Happy Satan's Birthday.
(I know, it makes no sense.)
He frowned a bit in the middle of his smile.
Then, in a second meeting, I farted while he was speaking, very loudly.

Both times he said that he agreed in principle with the demands but was limited in what he could achieve.

Unfortunately, authority is most believed.

It's so eminently believable that it's made many other things difficult to believe.

Everywhere someone interrogates someone else on how the misfortune in their life can't possibly be true.

Everywhere someone doesn't believe what their self is telling them about what they like or need.

Refusing to hear my own self in favour of authority.

Finding it difficult not only to refuse authority, but to believe in other people's fantasies.

Wanting to edit other people's fantasies. "I think this part can go" or "This is awkward."

When it takes absolute precision and courage to describe a fantasy.

My family enters the lottery every week.

We buy the same numbers each time, based on our birthdays.

The numbers marked in shiny carbon are
1 / 6 / 9 / 10 / 11 / 19

While we wait for the results, we break into a vacant building
with a group of our neighbours.

We paint the walls inside orange and lavender and silver and put
up green lights that tremble in time to the beat.

I accept talking with my mouth and tongue.
I accept talking with my ass.
I accept talking with my body.

I accept how other people show the truth to me.
I accept being shown.
I accept sensing.

QUIVERING ASS

Quivering ass of the world:

How does what pleases me
know that it pleases me?

Cropped patched sweater with mountain-lake-bird scene
and two different sleeves.

A flower that became a flower over time.
Determining on its own
its perfect shape and colour.

Flavour:
max astringency.

There is only one being, one thing.
It formed itself, initially, with the intention of being loved.

If I ask it to come here

it comes.

I take notes on all fours.

LUCKY GOURD

A doctor lives in a small gourd.

The doctor travels from town to town, harvesting and
giving out medicine.
When the doctor needs rest, she walks through the door of the
gourd, shrinking as she passes to four inches tall.
Once inside, she falls asleep tucked in a tiny bed.
There's a tiny tapestry of a mountain on the wall.

The gourd is shaped like a figure 8.
A gardener knew the doctor was coming.
They knew what was needed to make the gourd the right shape.
They prepared the soil and built a trellis out of sticks
so the gourd could grow, hanging,
into its final form.

Pushing out of the seed,
the vine grew in a spiral fashion.
At every moment it sensed which way to turn.
Pulling
water
and
sugar
up.
The vine knew when it could bear
its fruit's weight.

A SCREW

My mom asks me questions there are no answers for.

One of the arms of my glasses fell off, the tiny screw fell out, a
screw the size of a speck.
My mom cried, Where did it go?!
Why did it fall out?!
What did you do?!
She was upset and I thought, I'm never going to find it.

We were on a vacation.
We were on a bus shaking its way up a mountain
the $99 bus tour in China.
The screw was smaller than a piece of dust.
How would I know why screws get loose.
Why they fall out,
why they roll away.
I put my head against the bus window and closed my eyes
the glasses lopsided on my face.

Mom said, Don't worry I'll find it for you.
I sighed in frustration, petulant, Ya right, Mom.
The bus clattering up the mountain.
She put her head back on the headrest and closed her eyes and
began to pray.
Her lips moved in prayer.

Then she opened her eyes, got up from her seat, walked down
the shaking bus aisle, bent over and reached behind a metal seat
leg on the shuddering black rubber floor.

She came back with the tiny screw in her hand, smiling.
A gold speck in the middle of her palm.
The carved thread of the screw shining.

I realize that she asks the same questions of me and of God.
The asking is the reason.

WITH SWORD

A period of time during which the heart becomes comfortable
as the sword's sheath.
With sword.

All along the river:
long grasses.

Beside the river:
closed bookstore with only blue books.

The sunlight has bleached all the covers blue.
Steam Engine History, Organic Gardening, everything is the
same turquoise blue.
Light's energy breaks the molecular bonds of the dyes
causing the colours to fade.
Red absorbs more energy
and blue absorbs less.

This phenomenon of light is no different than the
telling of stories.
A teacher in grade school would always make fun of my shoes...
The grade school teacher was cruel and is still remembered as
such fifty-five years later.
The story about the shoes, told for the second time this month,
not told as if new, but as a retelling, to grow comfortable in.
The teacher's name is still said with the same feeling, but
pronounced in a slightly different way.
Like the vowels are a little bit longer and softer.

I learned about light from trying to paint a gourd.

Watch as the light hits the water.

Watch as the water breaks.

The bookstore's sign has a painting of a book's cover:
The title is *NOVEL* and the image is a rounded door.

A story is like a door not only because it's a passage but because
it takes time to build.

A door requires a frame and both have to be precise. The
two have to fit into each other to create a seal, plus there's the
element of gravity when hanging the hinges. So construction
can take a while.

Then, when it's finally done:
the door can slam open or shut.

It calls the will to move through it.

Faded handwritten sign pinned under a chair.

The water breaks itself.

Further along the river:
here is a person inspecting the soles of their shoes.
How one heel is worn down more than the other.

MOVIE OF MY LIFE

When the sun melts through the horizon everyone on the
mountaintop goes quiet.

To observe the red disc slipping over the brink.

To note the porousness of the limit.

Suddenly, a cloud of gnats gathers around someone. She waves
her hands but no use, the gnats flap their wings so hard that
they take off with her.
The gnats and the person fly off into the distance.

Now both the sun and the person are gone.
Everyone else is still silent.

On the mountaintop, I read that: *An overdevelopment of the logical brain can create challenges of autobiographical memory…*

Apparently this can happen when an expression of need is met with a lack of response.

This is because memories are created in states of presence. They can't be created in states of dissociation.

The logical brain tries to make the few memories that do exist line up straight.

A memory of my cousin giving me a book for my birthday.
He knew I loved to read and got me a novel titled *Flowers in the Attic* by V.C. Andrews. He must have grabbed it in a hurry from a supermarket check-out line.
It's a fucked-up novel about a mother who locks her children in an attic in order to get an inheritance.
She slowly poisons them.
The children have an incestuous relationship with each other.
I was turned on and horrified while reading it.
I worried about my parents accidentally finding the book.
I prayed that no one should ever know that I had read it.
So I took it to school in a plastic bag and threw it in the garbage bin in the girls' bathroom.

Another memory is of an assumption I had that my parents went out at night while my sister and I were asleep to do weird and fucked-up things for extra money.

Another memory is of a rule of how to behave around
other people.
The rule was:

Never tell anyone what you want.
Never describe exactly what you want.
Instead, you should move towards the opposite of what you want,
and then maybe someone will figure out what you want.

Another memory is of Poh-Poh's memory of war.

After she died, my mom texted me to ask, Do you have the recording of when you talked to Grandma about her life?

She said, I want to keep my mom's story.

The recording of Poh-Poh's life story is a series of facts that don't always connect.

As a child, she was almost taken to a convent by her mom who decided to become a nun, as refuge from the deaths of all the other children, but at the last minute, her stepsister decided to take care of her instead.

The recording doesn't describe what it felt like.

The pain or the joy.

At the recording's end, my poh-poh says,
Sometimes I remember and sometimes I don't. If I have
anything more to tell you, I will.

And in the moment of her transformation
she opened her eyes very wide and looked straight up at the
ceiling.

Back on the mountaintop, in the complete dark,
the gnats bring the person back. They put her down softly
and she brushes off her clothes, now covered in a pattern of
thousands of tiny holes. She is tired but happy.

Waterfall of my life.

Waterfall of our lives.

In our moments of transformation.

We will be dissolved in our own stories.

Unfurling into the source.

Eaten by the rocks.

NOTES

The Poet Li Bai
The poem by Li Bai is titled "Quiet Night Thought" [靜夜思].

Natural Fact
For colonial-era property systems in Hong Kong, see Cecilia Louise Chu, "Speculative Modern: Urban Forms and the Politics of Property in Colonial Hong Kong," (PhD diss., University of California, Berkeley), 2012, 27, https://escholarship.org/content/qt3r14d2r5/qt3r14d2r5_noSplash_a95ba480e3a0f2d131538d79303209be.pdf.

Protection
Adam Elenbaas, "Bhakti Wednesday: The Universal Form of God Part One," *Nightlight Astrology* podcast, October 20, 2021, https://www.youtube.com/watch?v=n-SjjjWOnw4&ab_channel=Acyuta-bhavaDas. The story is from the *Bhagavata Purana*, Volume Two, translated by Ramesh Menon.

Life's Not Fair
Carlo Ginzburg, *The Cheese and the Worms: The Cosmos of a Sixteenth-Century Miller*, Johns Hopkins University Press, [1976] 2013.

Door
Ron Tran, *Apartment #201*, 2008, artist's apartment door removed and displayed in the gallery for duration of exhibition, variable dimensions and objects, Künstlerhaus Bethanien, https://www.bethanien.de/en/artists/ron-tran/.

Autoicon
Donald Rodney, Geoff Cox, Mike Phillips, Eddie Chambers, Richard Hylton, Angelika Koechert, Virginia Nimarkoh, Keith Piper, Gary Stewart, Diane Symons, and Adrian Ward, *AUTOICON*, 2000, dynamic internet work and CD-ROM, Iniva, London, https://iniva.org/programme/projects/autoicon/. See also https://i-dat.org/autoicon/.

Donald Rodney, *Nine Night in Eldorado*, September 10 to October 12, 1997, South London Gallery, London, https://www.southlondongallery.org/exhibitions/donald-rodney-nine-night-in-eldorado/.

Donald Rodney, *Psalms*, 1997, autonomous wheelchair constructed with Guido Bugmann. See also https://i-dat.org/psalms/.

For Jeremy Bentham's Autoicon, see Chris Haffenden, "Every Man His Own Monument: Self-Monumentalizing in Romantic Britain," (PhD diss., Uppsala University), 2018, 40–91, https://www.semanticscholar.org/paper/Every-Man-His-Own-Monument-%3A-Self-Monumentalizing-Haffenden/7de601d5f974456fc7808571060f3cc34c8f8c6f.

Demands
Messages from Bhupen Khakhar, directed by Judy Marle (1983, British Film Institute), https://www.youtube.com/watch?v=tqz_fKZZDJg&ab_channel=BFI.

For Chinese oaths and perjury, see Christopher Munn, "The Criminal Trial Under Early Colonial Rule," *Hong Kong's History: State and society under colonial rule,* ed. Tak-Wing Ngo, Routledge, 1999, 60–61.

The photo on page 119 was taken by the author, at the apartment complex in Hong Kong where she lived as a baby.

ACKNOWLEDGEMENTS

Love and thanks to Marvin Luvualu António, Yuula Benivolski, Lauren Bride, Tina Guo, Sheila Heti, Jason Hirata, Oliver Husain, Onyeka Igwe, Steve Kado, Paul Kajander, HaeAhn Woo Kwon, Audrea Lim, Emerson Maxwell, Park McArthur, Dana Michel, Monica Moraru, Sean O'Neill, Aliya Pabani, Lily Jue Sheng, Margaux Williamson, Annie Wong, Nikki Woolsey, and Friends of Chinatown Toronto.

Love and thanks to my mom, my dad, my sister, Mike, and Benny.

Love and thanks to Robin "Cocobun" Simpson.

Thanks to my editors and readers, especially Bopha Chhay, River Halen, Samra Mayanja, Monica Moraru, and Robin Simpson. And many thanks to Alayna Munce, Brenda Leifso, and Rayzel Bermudez at Brick Books.

Thanks and solidarity to the Indigenous peoples on whose land I live and work: the Mississaugas of the Credit and other Anishinaabeg nations, the Haudenosaunee, and the Wendat.

Versions of some of these poems were published in *The Happy Hypocrite* (Book Works), *Interjection Calendar* (Montez Press), and in the chapbook *The Four Onions* (yolkless press). "Pink Outfit" was originally written for HaeAhn Woo Kwon's 2021 exhibition *Bathroom Classroom*.

Amy Ching-Yan Lam is an artist and writer. She makes exhibitions, performances, and public artworks. She was part of the duo Life of a Craphead from 2006 to 2020. Her book *Looty Goes to Heaven* was published in 2022. *Baby Book* is her first book of poetry. She lives in Tkaronto/Toronto and was born in Hong Kong.